THE MEETING PLACE
and Other Poems

(A Collection of Lyric Poems and Haiku)

G. Anita Johnson

ISBN: 1-4140-6143-9 (e-book)
ISBN: 1-4140-6142-0 (Paperback)

This book is printed on acid-free paper.

1stBooks – rev. 02/28/04

TABLE OF CONTENTS

Lyrics on Life

The Meeting Place

How often we meet
In this little room —
Both of us artists,
Or so we assume.

She stands at the printer,
The copier's mine.
We need to pay bills,
With a night out to dine.

A beautiful landscape
She paints with her brush
While I'll write a poem
When not in a rush.

How often we meet
In this little room.
The printer and copier
Both share our gloom.

No Picasso or Dali,
Monét or Renoir,
But the drone of the printer
We hear from afar.

How often we meet
In this little room —
An artist, a poet,
Or so we assume.

Perhaps we'll create
Our masterpiece yet
And the drone of the printer
We soon will forget!

G. Anita Johnson

In Search of Dawn

The lighthouse flickers
In search of Dawn . . .
It towers above the
Reckless waves
And snowcapped boulders,
Looming large against
The blackened night —
In search of Dawn.
It beckons to the army
Of the heavens
To form a militia
In search of Dawn.
But night quietly passes
As Dawn appears stealthily
On the horizon —
Luminous, sedate,
Well-rested from the night,
Ready and willing
To face the day at hand.

A Man of Distinction

He looks so suave and debonair
White crested waves of wispy hair
With laugh lines reaching to the skies
His lips curl up in tasteful lies.

While Mother Age pursues his face
Grandfather Wealth has kept apace
So well preserved, this stately form
Has weathered life's untimely storm.

Impeccable his style of dress –
A false façade of true finesse
To sign a contract, close a deal
Imprint a legalistic seal.

Of such distinction is the man
He seeks to change the Master plan
Yet he, like those beneath the grave,
Not one of humankind can save.

G. Anita Johnson

Buildings of Stone

So many buildings of stone
So many people they house
Still lies a man all alone
None can his spirit arouse.

He played his music each night
Opened his window in song
They closed the door ever tight
Hoping he wouldn't be long.

So many buildings of stone
So many people they hold
Here lies a man all alone
Here lies a body so cold.

Why does a building of stone
Shelter so many, yet few
How can a building of stone
Give such a man his just due?

Tower Power

The WTC was known to be
A force for peace and unity,
The Finance Center of the world
Where nations could their flag unfurl.

Its towers graced the skies above
Which New York and the world did love
Where visitors from far and wide
Admired the view from every side.

But then the blast of 9-11
Did echo through the gates of heaven,
Its message spewed up hate and fear
That Armageddon could be near.

Three thousand lives or more were lost
So precious — who could count the cost?
Our dear ones and our heroes, too,
Were silenced by a frenzied few.

And still the winds of fire and ash
Remind us of that thund'rous clash,
Of jet-fueled fires, glass and steel,
Of devastation so surreal.

Twin towers of titanic might
Were banished from our cherished sight
As black clouds painted night on day
And visions turned to ash and clay.

But our strength lies not in those towers;
Another source our soul empowers,
The power of humanity
For here we stand, a people free.

G. Anita Johnson

Reflections on a porch

A house without a porch, I say?
To prominently thus display
A couch of quiet, sweet repose
For angels e'en to rest, who knows?
To ponder thoughts in solitude
Or seek a treasured interlude
From mundane tasks of everyday
Perchance to rest, perchance to pray.

A house without a porch? Touché.
Imagine what a porch might say —
Its stately posts would bear sweet tales
Of sipping noontime ginger ales.
Its timbers echo "safe retreat"
To shade one from the sultry heat.
Perhaps a flower box or two
Add fragrance and a vintage view.

A house without a porch, I say?
My instant thought is pure dismay.
No place to offer peace of mind
To travelers of the weary kind.
No more a butterfly's retreat;
No more a place where lovers meet
To reminisce the days gone by —
To touch, to kiss, perhaps to cry.

A house without a porch, I say?
My prompt response would thus be "nay."

Bottom of the Barrel

Have you ever felt
You reached the
Bottom of the barrel
When there were no
More words left
To express your sorrow
And no more hope
For a new tomorrow.

But then you heaved
A heavy sigh
And found one more breath
To give life
To your existence
To reach out for happiness
To aspire to the stars.

You hadn't reached the
Bottom of the barrel
After all
But had only broken
Your fall
From high heaven
To humble earth.

G. Anita Johnson

awakenings

a seedling sprouts from a blanket of warm, loving earth
caressed by torrid, nurturing sun-rays,
dripping dew drops of sweet elixir,
awakened by Spring's rebuttal to Winter's deadly frost.

a romance blooms in the shade of a white magnolia,
warm, almond eyes caressing pomegranate lips,
melting with sweet elixir,
awakened by dormant memories of Love's wintry frost.

an old man reminisces of years gone by
when he kissed his bride beneath the white magnolia,
the pungent aroma of blossoms filling the air –
but his eyes are closed by Death's sweet elixir
until the time when he is awakened by
Resurrection's rebuttal to Winter's deadly frost.

Outcry

It makes you feel worth less
than two small sparrows

You walk the dead end road
that winds and narrows

Into a chamber dark
Of constant harrows.

G. Anita Johnson

Night Falls

The weary sun takes a rear seat
In the Galactic theater
As night falls.
First on stage – the moon
In her nocturnal glory.
Rising to heavenly bliss,
She peers into the darkness
While glistening stars adorn her
With their celestial acts.

I hear Mozart's Requiem
Playing in the distance
As night falls.
How artfully the notes rise and fall
To the rhythm of my heartbeat,
A heart so heavy with
Nocturnal gloom,
Too heavy to notice the night's
Performance upon the
Galactic stage.

Time

Its corridors are fraught with plaintiff cries
Of heroes echoing their last goodbyes
No treasured moment captured in a cast,
The present – once the future – now is past.

No man of mortal flesh can e'er descend
Its pedestals from alpha to the end
For only the Creator can foresee
What the omega e'er will prove to be.

For no one born of flesh has come to know
When time was born or whither it does go.
It marches ever onward in a stream
In oneness like a garment without seam.

For time indefinite our hearts do yearn
That the Almighty's wisdom we might learn
For ever we shall seek yet never find
The secrets that belie the quest of time.

G. Anita Johnson

The Wings of Time

They say that time flies
So where are its wings?
If time were a bird
It surely would sing

An aria sweet
Which none could compare
Then gently retreat,
Its wings in the air.

A Sonnet on Man

Youth treads in innocence upon the path
Of ageless time engraved in grains of sand
Which touch upon the patience and the wrath
But fail to further on this theme expand.
Men change this sand, this path which bore youth's pace
To meet their boundless quest to surpass time,
The infinite, which governs man's own race
To be the first to hear that unknown chime.

The aged tread once more upon that earth
And reminisce the innocent, the wise —
While endlessly they search for joy and mirth
That youth withheld, that wisdom would disguise.

So time goes on and each one will demand
The right to leave his imprint in the sand.

G. Anita Johnson

The Man With the Rose

He promenades Fifth Avenue
With rose in outstretched hand
As the aroma leads him to
A paradisaic land.

He answers not the biddings of
The horse-and-carriage men
For the man with the rose is riding
Where the horse has never been.

He dreams of sweet narcissus,
A psychedelic breeze,
While really it's his image,
A reflection that he sees.

So the man with the rose is riding
With gallantry of old
To the villages of maidens
Whose stories go untold.

Life is like a wildflower . . .

Life is like a wildflower
Growing freely in the grass
Having such a gay affair
Till at least the summer's past.
Then the autumn leaves abound
Proudly dancing 'round its bed
To the song of frosty death
Till the flower bows its head.

Life is like a wildflower
Reaching for the noontime sun
Chatting with the butterflies
Till the day is almost done.
Just when it has closed its eyes
For a bit of noonday rest
Lo a child would stumble by
Picking flowers at their best.

So is life a wildflower
Having its heyday
Till the scorching rays of time
Wither it away.

G. Anita Johnson

Just Remember Me When I Die

The widow kind of Zarephath
Whose flour and oil did not run out
We remember although she did die.

And like Dickinson, Emily,
I want your love posthumously.
Just remember me when I die.

Don't cry and shout or skip about,
Don't bow your head or puff and pout.
Just remember me when I die.

I'm not a Maya Angelou,
A Stromberg or a Figaro,
Just remember me when I die.

Lyrics on Love

You and I

I am the wind that knows not when to stay or go;
You are the sky that lights a way for me to know.

I am the wave who rides her love forever more;
You are the sea whose love will touch the farthest shore.

I am the brook that babbles forth so free and gay;
You are the nook that hides me on a stormy day.

I am the sun that's late into the early morn;
You are the moon that waits until the day is worn.

I am the dream that comes to you within the night;
You are the voice that wakens me at morning light.

G. Anita Johnson

We Used to Dance

O how I long for but a glance
A hint of starry eyed romance
A moment's view of how we used to dance.

My hand you held close by the fire
And talked of all our hearts' desire
A gentle kiss would all my love inspire.

We reached the pinnacle of life
We struggled through and coped with strife
I was much more to you than just your wife.

I was the apple of your eyes
The star that glimmered in your skies
A kitten in your arms that softly cries.

We laughed and played and took a chance
You filled each night with sweet romance
My heart now yearns for how we used to dance.

Hole in My Heart

Is there really a hole in my heart
In a place where I no longer feel
Is there really a hole in my heart
Has the pain been unable to heal?

What lies buried in crevices deep
In the fathomless depths of the sea?
Is there really a hole in my heart?
What is whole is what I'll never be.

G. Anita Johnson

Till the moon is no more

Till the moon is no more
Love is here
Tho the sea leaves the shore
I'll be there
To love you and keep you
And hold you in my arms.
Till the moon is no more
Love is here.

Till the moon is no more
Love is ours
Tho the clouds fail to send
April showers
I'll love you and hold you
And keep you with my charms
Till the moon is no more
Love is ours.

Not for just one lonely night
Love is here to stay.
Just like homing birds aflight
We will fly away.

Thank You

Thank you for changing the hands of time
Thank you for being a friend of mine.

You were thought to be so unkind
Others felt your wrath
But you proved you're a friend of mine
In the aftermath.

Thank you for putting in overtime
Thank you for making our voices chime.

We were just passing ships in time
Through the stormy years
But when my ship veered off its line
Your ship calmed my fears.

Thank you for being a friend of mine.
Thank you for changing the hands of time.

G. Anita Johnson

Inside

Inside – your love
Within my memory.
Inside – your love
Is what you shared with me.

Why did you have to go?
Now you will never know
Inside the love will always be.

Inside – your love
We had no words to speak.
Inside – your love
Your laughter now I seek.

You said no soft good-byes
As teardrops filled my eyes.
Inside the love will always be.

Inside – your love
Always within my mind.
Inside – your love
To seek but never find.

Why did you have to go?
Now you will never know
Inside the love will always be.

hurting

deeper than the black abyss
sharper than a serpent's hiss
hidden but awry, amiss –
yes, hurting

still he passes in the night
like a homing bird aflight
guided by a distant light –
forgotten

so he thinks that time will heal
all the wounds his daggers deal
none would dare to make appeal –
while hurting. . .

enter in the blackest hole
none escape its magnet pole
ne'er could light reveal the soul
who's hurting.

G. Anita Johnson

I'm Ready

You came into my life
And now I'm ready

My steps were so unsure
But now they're steady

The happiness you share
Has drowned my sorrow

And now I'm ready for
Each new tomorrow.

The Look

As fleeting as a perfumed scent
That lingers in the Autumn air
As piercing as the womb that's rent
By child aborted in despair,

The meeting of our eyes in truth
Belie the words of amity
Predicting as the sayer-sooth
An ending of calamity.

G. Anita Johnson

Repeat Performance

He dances at my door once more
And plays for me a timely score.
He knows of my dejected state,
That love for me has come too late.

Emotions ever shattered, torn,
The notes I hear as tainted scorn
Yet still he plays his melody
As if a tune would set me free.

A captive of a foreign land,
Upon its shores my heart does stand,
My feelings frozen — no repeat
Performance will my life replete.

No Guarantees

You've gotta take a chance for love
But there's no guarantee
You e'en could ride the clouds above
But there's no guarantee.

Now love may stay, and love may go
But there's no guarantee
If you don't try, you'll never know
But there's no guarantee.

Now I can't say I'll never break
Your heart or make you cry
But I sure want that flame to spark
No guarantees, just try.

I know it's you

I know it's you
Who played our song
In just a single note
I'd never get it wrong.

Just yesterday
You walked away
You turned the key
You sang so long.

I know it's you
That played our song
You played it on the beach
As waves would dance along.

And now we touch
The sands of time
I hold the notes
You left behind.

Who played that song
Who played that melody
Just took one note
To break the harmony.

I know it's you
You played it wrong.
I know it's you
That played our song.

A thousand nights of love

A thousand nights of love, now he's alone
With melodies of silence on his mind,
A thousand times romances he has known
But vanity in love his heart does find.
'Tis but a single focus, his request,
To share his lifelong dreams forever more.
The fire in his bones shall never rest
'Till waves of passion dance upon his shore.

Yet Solomon in all his wise grandeur
Among a thousand hearts had not unveiled
A love that's ever true, a love that's pure.
In company with kings, he, too, has failed.

Men great and small, a thousand loves have known.
The greater and the lesser die alone.

G. Anita Johnson

Your Face

Your face — what's the best part
of your face, you say.
Is it your boyish grin
that somehow my heart did win
or perhaps your dark bedroom eyes
that woo me in the shadows of —
your face — what's the best part
of your face?
Could it be the lines in your forehead
like the roots of a tree
that tell a story of mystery?
Or perhaps your nose
like 'a bridge over troubled waters' goes!
(That was supposed to be funny.)
You say, no, honey, you want the truth
not tomorrow, today — okay.
The best part of your face, I'd say,
is that which belongs to me, my love,
and you are mine forever to keep
so close your eyes and go to sleep —
that's the best part of your face.

Portrait of love in a clouded sky

Your love is with me always
from sunrise to sunset
beaming from the sky of eternity.

Even when the dark clouds
try to drown our love
with tears of discontent
still I feel the warmth
of your gentle rays.

And at sunrise
when your beaming face
appears in the dawning sky
I smile to know that
even maudlin teardrops
were but an interlude
in the current of our love
continuous as night flows into day
rejoicing subtly
as a flower unfolds
its petaled arms to kiss
the jeweled raindrops
that fall from a clouded sky.

G. Anita Johnson

They Say

They say it's better to have loved and lost
Than never to have loved someone at all
But I would rather by the sea be tossed
Than climb into the clouds and then to fall.
The fall is hard, the pain cuts deep inside.
You stutter and feel faint from lack of sleep.
Unsteady as the ebbing of the tide,
Your heart behind a mask you try to keep.

A fire in your bones begins to burn
Then comes relief in stupefying dreams.
A song is even difficult to learn
Or so within your memory it seems.

'Tis better to have never loved at all
Than climb into the clouds and then to fall.

the hole in the donut

A man walks in the rain —
drip by drip; he listens.
He touches the raindrops
one by one; he smiles.

A woman walks in the rain —
drop by drop; she listens.
The rain caresses her fingertips
inch by inch; she smiles.

A man and a woman walk in the rain —
drip by drop; they listen.
The rain speaks to them
patter by patter; they laugh.

A man and a woman have parted —
one by one; they walk.
The sun has lighted them a way
each by each; they remember
the hole in the donut.

G. Anita Johnson

The Kindred Spirit

Like delicate blades of grass
breaking through the concrete cracks,
reaching out to touch
the sun's warm, tender fingers —

Two hearts pulsate
to the rhythmic beat of moody blues,
and intertwine with the universe,
becoming one in thought and mind.

The kindred spirit blossoms between us
exulting to find its image
mirrored in a warm smile,
a quickened glance.

The kindred spirit reaches out
forever caring, sensitive, understanding
as the sea beckons the horizon
and joins hands in subliminal peace.

perchance

i, a blade of grass
waiting in the shadows
of his face, the moon,
encircled by flirting stars
so bright —
yet i, a humble blade of grass —
perchance that
his midnight beams
would shine upon me —
perchance . . .

i, shimmering in the dew
feel the warmth
of his moonlit glance
but then, as dawn
approaches her throne
he follows her
behind a gloomy cloud
leaving me to be
scorched by the sun,
a humble blade of grass,
undone.

G. Anita Johnson

There Is Love

With each breath that is breathed
with each sigh that is heaved
somewhere there is love.

With each note that is sung
from the tiniest lung
it vibrates with love.

Have you never been told
whether you're young or old
within you there's love.

If you have then you know
that God's spirit will glow
when you're walking in love.

Lyrics on Faith

Be Still

Be still, my sweet,
Don't rush your feet
Just wait upon your God.

Your time will come,
Now walk, don't run,
The way the Master trod.

It seems uphill
But just be still
And keep a steady pace.

The battle is
Not yours, but his.
Be still and do not chafe.

G. Anita Johnson

You Are Not Alone

You think you're on your own
But you are not alone
For there's a hand beside you
And holy spirit guides you.

For our Great God above
Has wrapped us all in love.
He shapes us as our Potter
That we may never totter.

Of Moses

O Father of celestial lights,
Maker of the heavenly nights,
Who lifts his eyes to see your smile
As Moses on the River Nile.

You guided him to Pharaoh's shore
But taught him well to love you more
Than riches or a kingly prize
That on your Christ he keep his eyes.

And though reproach he bore within
That humble slaves were next of kin,
Humility then made him great,
Exalted to a princely state;
The meekest of all men by far,
A prophet like the morning star.

To him you gave your sacred Word
That praises to your name be heard
Yet once he failed to walk your path
And thus invoked your iron wrath;
His heart's desire you then denied,
Before the Promised Land he died.

Yet in your memory he'll live
For sin and error you forgive
That all your loyal ones may rise
To fill the earthly paradise.

G. Anita Johnson

Ode to the God of Loyal Love

How great your loving kindness and
Your mercies to us all
You guided Lot to safety when
Gomorrah's gates did fall,

Gave Abraham the wisdom to
His servant send away
To find a wife for Isaac 'mongst
His brothers, he did pray.

Your loyal love did reach the cell
Of Joseph in despair,
Exalted him to Pharaoh's court
That food stuffs he'd prepare.

Your loyal love produced a Seed
Of promise as foretold
That we may have true faith to see
Your purposes unfold.

Ode to the Rock

O look within my heart, dear God,
And spare me not your iron rod
That words of truth fore'er I speak
And praise of men I never seek.

But always in the path of right
I take my steps and keep my sight
That I may walk at your command
And keep your love and hold your hand.

O Jah, my Rock, my Hope, my Sight,
Hear my prayers within the night
When tears give way to faith and hope
And fearful in the dark I grope,
Correct my thoughts and mold my mind
That once again your peace I find
And at the dawn I wake to see
Your spirit hover over me.

Alas, my God, my Hope, my Might,
The Rock, indeed, for truth and right,
Draw close your comforts of the night
That joy may sprout at morning light.

G. Anita Johnson

Ode to the Maker of Heaven and Earth

O praise Jehovah, our God and King,
May every voice his glory sing,
O praise the Maker of heaven and earth
And tell his truth with joy and mirth.

For He gives life when undeserved
And peace and love when He is served
By those whose hearts are pure and kind,
By those who bow with humble mind.

That earth and sea and wind may laugh
And river and spring and mountain path
To praise the Maker of heaven and earth
And sing his truth with joy and mirth.

A Voice in Ramah

I hear a voice cry out in pain
That all her children have been slain
Their slaughter bears the mark of Cain
That sons would never more remain.

G. Anita Johnson

Hezekiah's Prayer

King Hezekiah prayed and God did grant
More years of life, fifteen, that he might know
How frail we humans are, our knowledge scant.
Humility and faith we e'er must show.

His kingly tears and earnest pleadings, heard
By the Almighty One, our Sovereign Lord,
His fears of the Assyrian were curbed;
In God's own might he conquered Satan's horde.

Thus from his bed of sickness he did rise
And asked a sign be given that proved true.
The shadow did retreat before his eyes;
This only God Jehovah could e'er do.

Yes, Hezekiah prayed that he might live
And fifteen years of peace his God did give.

"Hush! Be Quiet!"

O "Hush! Be quiet!" were words Christ spoke
When holy spirit he invoked
To still the waters and the wind
That stirred the hearts of men who sinned.

These men did fear for life and breath
That stormy seas would mark their death.
The wind enraged that stormy sea,
Those waters they called Galilee.

O "Hush! Be quiet!" was Christ's rebuke.
As penned by his disciple Luke,
He calmed the seas as men did cower.
Who was this man of awesome power?

O how we yearn to see the day
When earth and wind and sea obey.
No stormy seas will e'er withstand
The kingly voice of Christ's command.

G. Anita Johnson

Reflections on Malawi - 1975

Bewildered and confused he humbly stands
Upon the border of an alien ground,
A refugee. In two undistant lands
His people by an iron yoke are bound.
He has no flag of country to unfurl
So ask him not to pledge his party choice.
His citizenship lies not in this world;
Till death he'll serve Jehovah and rejoice.

A letter from Dzaleka brings a tear —
His wife and child at Dowa have arrived.
Frelimo's yoke he'd rather have to bear
Than learn that those he loves have not survived.

Malawi, how his heart cries out for you,
"Forgive them, for they know not what they do."

A name to time indefinite

A name to time indefinite
Is what our God will give
To those who for the Kingdom's sake
In singleness will live.

'Tis not a noose to put about
Your neck or make you chafe,
But those who can make room for it
Will keep the 'kingdom' safe.

If you would cultivate the gift
And keep a settled heart,
Desires of the flesh resist
Right from the very start.

Instead give of yourself to those
Who need encouragement
And you'll receive the greater joy,
A gift that's heaven sent.

A life free from anxiety
And all those worldly cares,
Without distraction from the Lord,
Made powerful by prayers.

A eunuch for the Kingdom's sake,
A blessed state can be
If on Jehovah you rely
And keep integrity.

G. Anita Johnson

A Time and a Place

A time and a place we have today
As good times we enjoy;
A time and a place to keep, we pray,
As God's Word we employ.

A time and a place we seek to gain
With eyes fixed on the prize;
We long for the end of death and pain —
A peaceful paradise.

For now is the time to seek to find
Jehovah's way of truth,
By serving our God with heart and mind
Forever, from our youth.

A time and a place for young and old
The Kingdom first to seek,
By making Jehovah our stronghold
And proving we are meek.

A time and a place for every voice
To join in Kingdom song,
By making a dedicated choice —
To whom do you belong?

Remember this world will pass away,
A time and place no more.
God's Kingdom will everlasting stay
A time and place for sure.

Lyrics on Nature

O Look What You Have Made

The velvet touch of the petaled leaves,
The quiet hush of an autumn breeze,
The gentle kiss of an April shower,
The peaceful bliss of the dawning hour.

O look what you have made . . .

The dew-dropped peaks of Mount Hermon's slope,
The graceful leaps of the antelope,
The cutting edge of a grassy blade,
The cooling breath of the summer shade,
The starry glance of the midnight sky,
The perfect form of the naked eye.

O look what you have made . . .

Who sets the limits of your command,
Who guides the stylus within your hand,
Who etched the rainbow upon the sky,
Who raised the mountains to stand on high?

Not one that you have made.

G. Anita Johnson

O Candelabra
(Brazilian Pine Tree)

You stand with outstretched arms to praise
Your Grand Creator all your days
O Candelabra, tree of pine
With branches of unique design.

This pine of wood such value told
That some of men have called it "gold"
With roots within Brazilian soil
Which man with ax in hand did spoil.

Few of your kind remain today,
Preserved by the azure jay
Which feeds upon *pinhões*, seeds,
Stored in the moss and deadened trees.

Can humans, yet of higher mind,
Be your preservers of like kind
And save the Candelabra tree
For generations yet to be?

The Wind

A man of many faces – the wind,
Sometimes so soft and shy,
Hiding behind the corner of a building
And then wisping out so gaily
To meet the passersby.

He laughs and frolics with the
Autumn leaves and scampers through
Litter on city streets.
Awesomely he meets the challenge
Of winter – bold and breathtaking,
A man of courage.

How shamefully he turns about
When winter turns to spring
As if he were envious of her beauty.
He howls and wrestles with the
Budding branches, marching boldly
Through open lots in a stirring rage.

But then, as if by some miracle,
April's tears abate him and he quiets
Like a kitten. So soft and cuddly
He waits until a blustery day when
He wants to be noticed as
A man of many faces – the wind.

G. Anita Johnson

Snow

Its form is white and crystalline
While falling from on high
With beauty that can ne'er be matched,
A marvel in the sky.

It saturates the earth below
And fills the mighty seas;
It covers trees with coats of lace
And flutters in the breeze.

O who can match its blueprints or
Describe its pattern true?
A feat beyond the works of men
That only God could do.

Reflections

The crested waves play
A timeless melody against
The jagged rocks —
Soothing and smoothing them
To perfection.

The ocean roars
In a jealous rage
Reeking havoc and deflection.

The calming seas
Kiss the noontime sun —
A small child studies
His reflection.

Haiku

Trees

Elegant trees
Riding the backs of mountains
Fallen leaves.

G. Anita Johnson

Summer

Summer's song
Birds singing lullabies
Autumn sleeps.

Stars

Twinkling stars
Sending their Morse code messages
Jealous moon.

G. Anita Johnson

Clouds

Nimbus clouds
Puffed like soiled white pillows
Stars asleep.

Snowflakes

Snowflakes fall
Crystalline and pure
Autumn weeps.

G. Anita Johnson

Fast Food

Melted arch
Hump-backed like hungry camels
Burger and fries.

Staircase

Climbing steps
Zigzagging throughout life
Heaven waits.

ABOUT THE AUTHOR

Author G. Anita Johnson has been developing her craft of poetry since the age of 14. Her poems have been published in several journals and anthologies, and she has received numerous poetry awards. Ms. Johnson's writing sparkles with vivid imagery, keen imagination, and deep emotion that will capture the hearts of her readers. Her first book of poetry, *Journeys* (Rutledge 2002), has been described as "a book to treasure". Ms. Johnson's goal in writing focuses on uplifting, nourishing and comforting the human spirit. She teaches Bible education and also enjoys traveling and interior decorating. Ms. Johnson is a native of Staten Island and currently resides there with her family.

www.ingramcontent.com/pod-product-compliance
Lightning Source LLC
Chambersburg PA
CBHW020354290526
45785CB00005B/2287